AMAZING FRACTIONS

ACTIVITY BOOK FOR CHILDREN

Observe and write the fraction of the circled monkeys.

$$\frac{2}{6}$$

Write fractions of the colored part.

$$\frac{}{}$$

Circle the butterflies according to the colored portion.

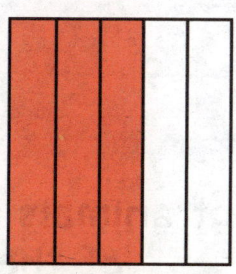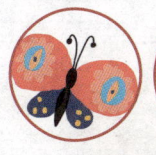

Write the fraction of the colored part on the orange.

a.

$$\frac{}{}$$

b.

$$\frac{2}{8}$$

c.

$$\frac{}{}$$

d.

$$\frac{3}{8}$$

Wonder House

Fractions Fun

Fractions is a numerical value that represents the equal parts of a whole. Each fraction has a numerator and a denominator.

The numerator tells us the number of parts out of total. The denominator tells us the parts in total.

numerator
$$\frac{3}{4}$$
denominator

Make fractions using the given numbers.

Numerators	Denominators	Fraction
a. 3	5	—
b. 5	8	—
c. 6	10	—
d. 7	9	—

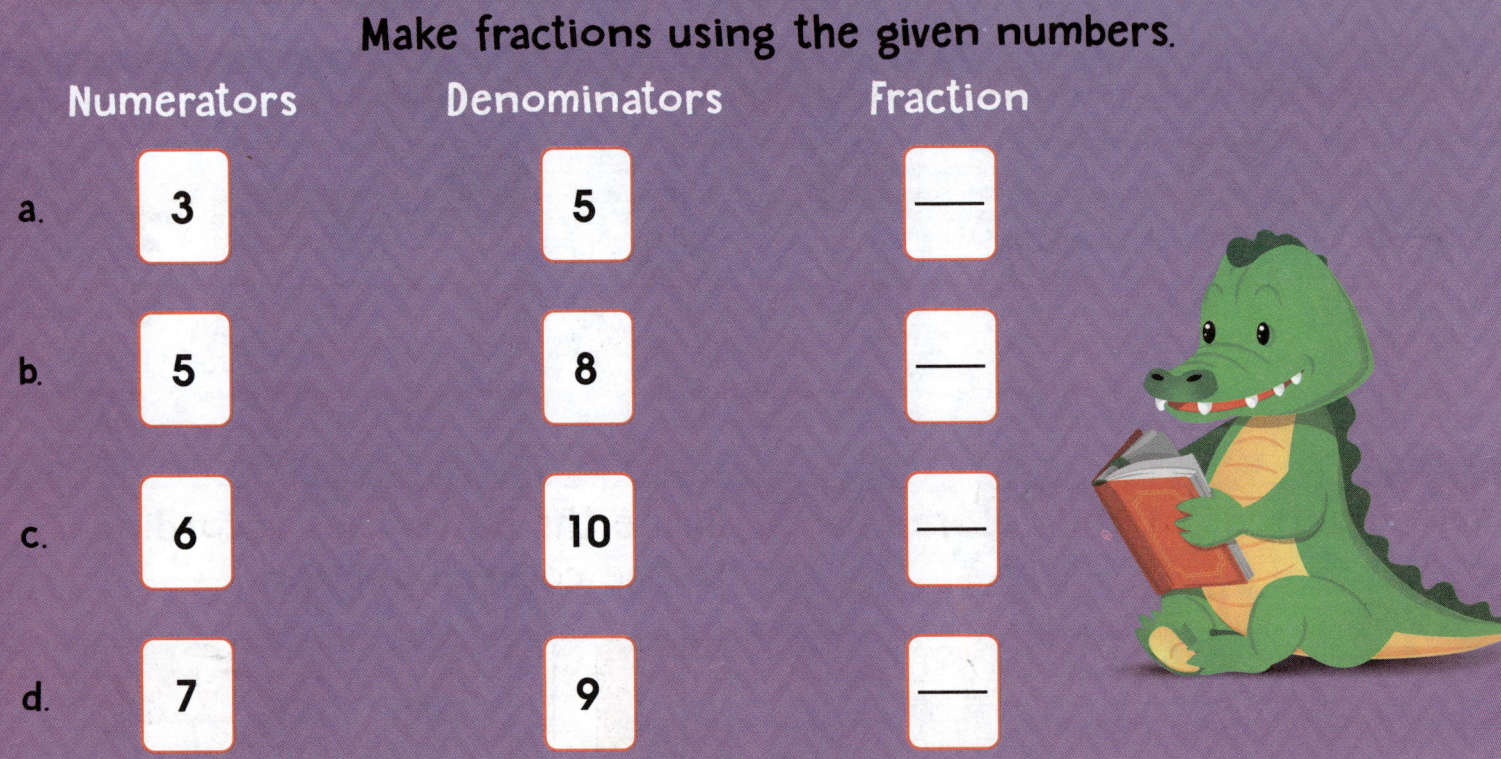

Circle the number of animals according to the colored portion of the fraction.

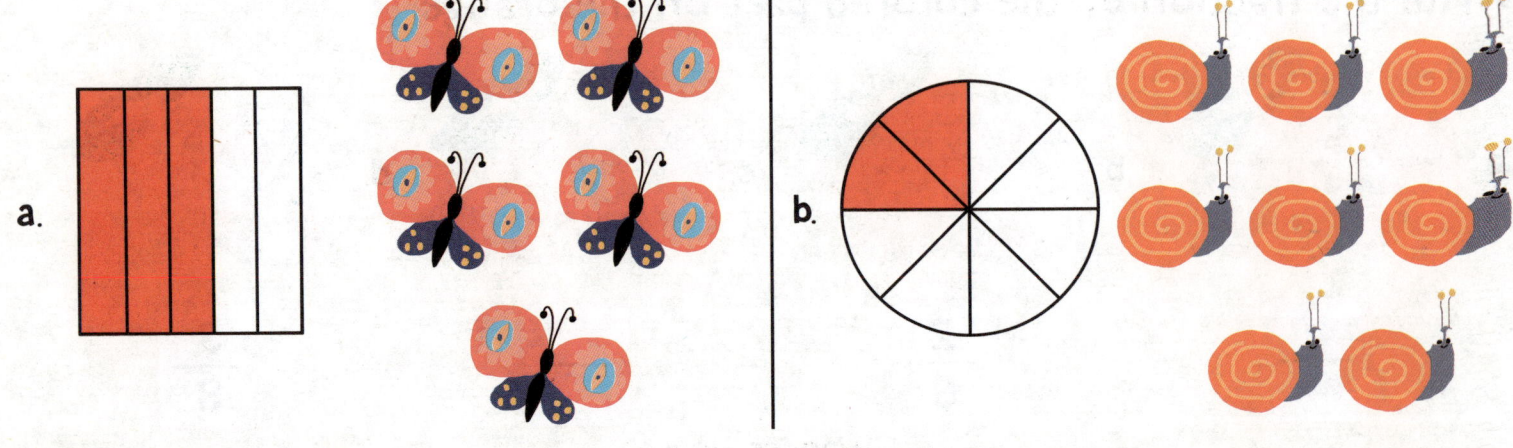

a.

b.

Name the Fraction Part

Identify the numerator and denominator.

a. In the fraction $\frac{3}{6}$, 6 is the _____

b. In the fraction $\frac{2}{7}$, 2 is the _____

c. In the fraction $\frac{1}{3}$, 3 is the _____

d. In the fraction $\frac{2}{8}$, 8 is the _____

e. In the fraction $\frac{3}{5}$, 3 is the _____

Draw a figure representing the fraction $\frac{5}{7}$.

All Kinds of Shapes

Color the shapes according to the given fractions.

a.

$\frac{3}{4}$ Three by Four

b.

$\frac{2}{4}$ Two by Four

c.

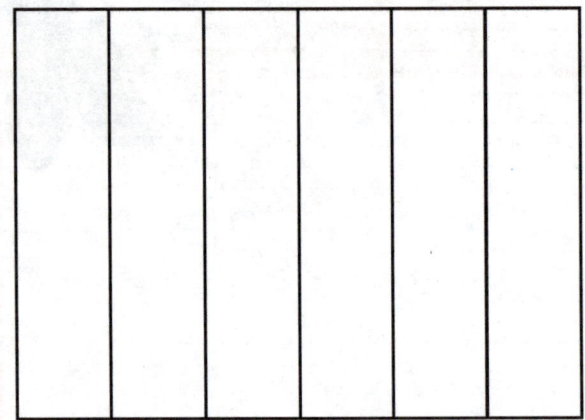

$\frac{4}{6}$ Four by Six

d.

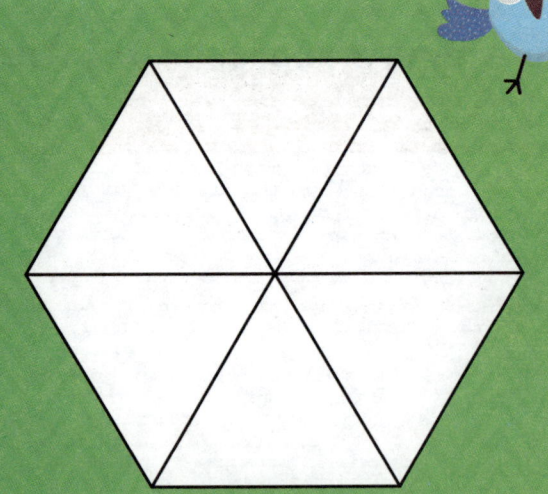

$\frac{5}{6}$ Five by Six

Color Fractions

Write fractions of the colored part.

a.  $\dfrac{2}{5}$

b.

c.

d.

e.

Coloring Fun

Color the objects as per the given fractions.

a.  $\dfrac{2}{3}$

b.  $\dfrac{2}{5}$

c.  $\dfrac{3}{4}$

d.  $\dfrac{2}{5}$

Match and Color

Match the figures on the Left with their fraction written in numerals and in words on the right.

a.  •

$\frac{1}{3}$

• One fourth

b.  •

$\frac{1}{6}$

• One fifth

c.  •

$\frac{1}{5}$

• One Sixth

d. 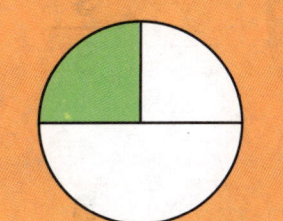 •

$\frac{1}{4}$

• One third

Choose the correct figure and color it in the fraction of 3/4.

a.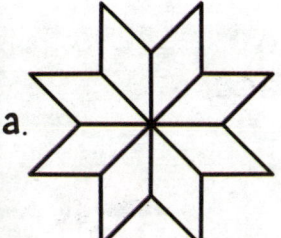

b.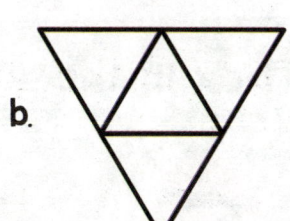

c.

d.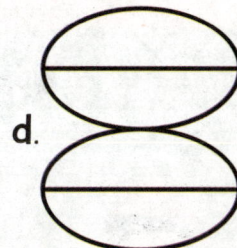

e.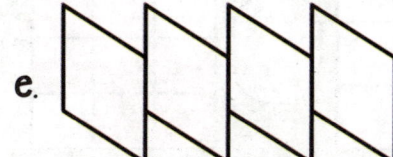

f.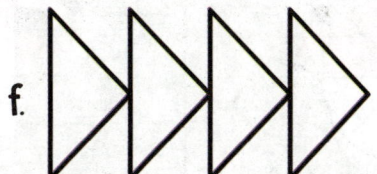

g.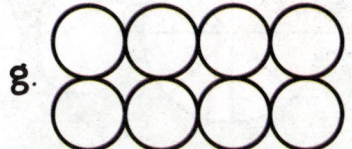

Going in Circles

Circle the fraction that matches the colored part of the figure.

a.

$\frac{5}{8}$

$\frac{3}{8}$

$\frac{2}{8}$

b.

$\frac{4}{8}$

$\frac{2}{8}$

$\frac{1}{8}$

c.

$\frac{3}{8}$

$\frac{6}{8}$

$\frac{5}{8}$

d.

$\frac{6}{8}$

$\frac{3}{8}$

$\frac{5}{8}$

Which fraction is bigger? Put > or < in the given space.

a.
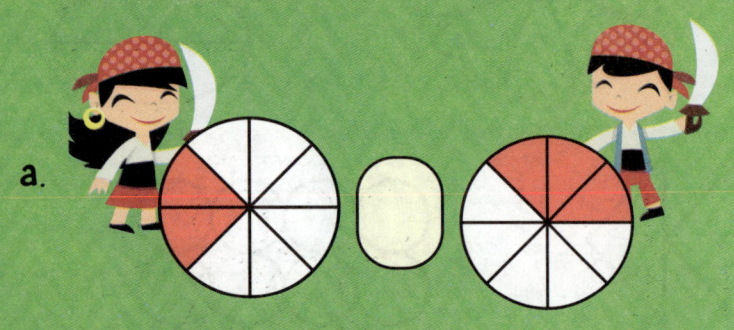

b.

What's the Count?

Circle the number of animals according to the colored portion of the figures.

a.

b.

c.

d.

Which is Greater?

Which fraction is bigger? Put >, < or = in the given space.

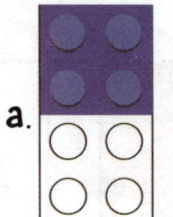 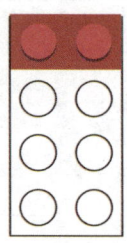

a. $\dfrac{4}{8}$ ◯ $\dfrac{2}{8}$

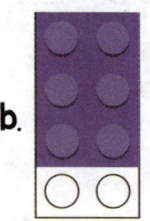 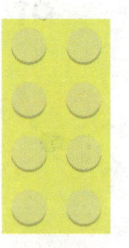

b. $\dfrac{6}{8}$ ◯ $\dfrac{8}{8}$

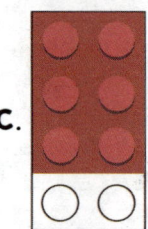 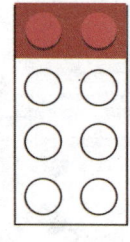

c. $\dfrac{6}{8}$ ◯ $\dfrac{2}{8}$

 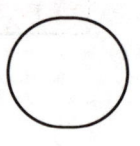

d. $\dfrac{2}{8}$ ◯ $\dfrac{3}{8}$

 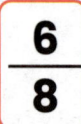

e. $\dfrac{8}{8}$ ◯ $\dfrac{4}{8}$

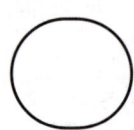 

f. $\dfrac{2}{8}$ ◯ $\dfrac{8}{8}$

 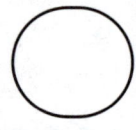 
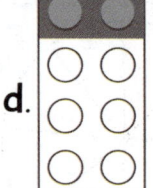 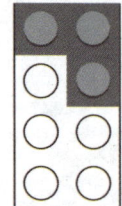 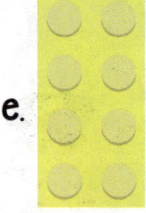
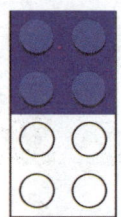  
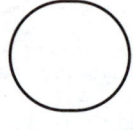 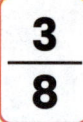 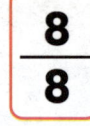 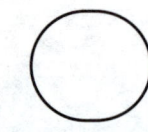  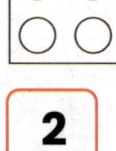 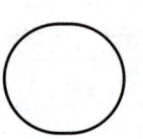

a. $\dfrac{6}{7}$ ◯ $\dfrac{2}{7}$

b. $\dfrac{1}{12}$ ◯ $\dfrac{9}{12}$

c. $\dfrac{6}{6}$ ◯ $\dfrac{5}{6}$

d. $\dfrac{1}{3}$ ◯ $\dfrac{3}{3}$

 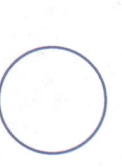 
 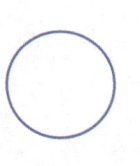 
 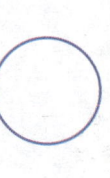 
 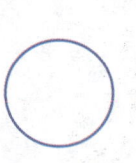 

Adding Fractions

Add the given fractions.

a.  $\dfrac{3}{5}$ + $\dfrac{1}{5}$ =

b. $\dfrac{1}{6}$ +  $\dfrac{3}{6}$ =

c.  $\dfrac{5}{7}$ +  $\dfrac{2}{7}$ =

d. $\dfrac{3}{8}$ +  $\dfrac{2}{8}$ =

Count and Write

Count the colored circles and write the fraction.

a. ___

b. ___

c. ___

d. ___

e. ___

f. ___

Put the given fractions in order on the number Lines.

a. $\dfrac{1}{2}$, $\dfrac{3}{2}$, $\dfrac{5}{2}$, $\dfrac{2}{2}$, $\dfrac{4}{2}$

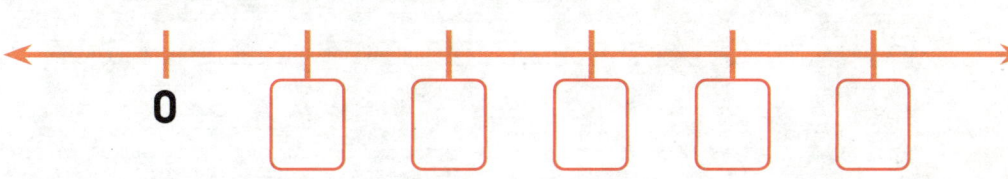

0

b. $\dfrac{6}{4}$, $\dfrac{3}{4}$, $\dfrac{5}{4}$, $\dfrac{2}{4}$, $\dfrac{4}{4}$, $\dfrac{1}{4}$

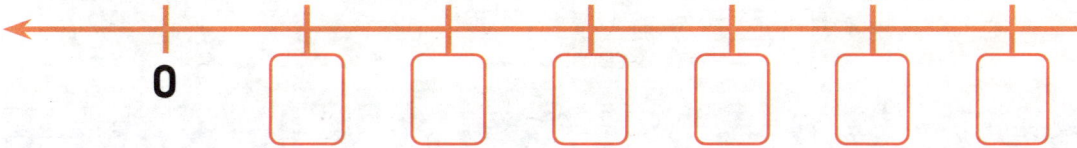

0

c. $\dfrac{6}{5}$, $\dfrac{3}{5}$, $\dfrac{7}{5}$, $\dfrac{2}{5}$, $\dfrac{4}{5}$, $\dfrac{5}{5}$, $\dfrac{1}{5}$

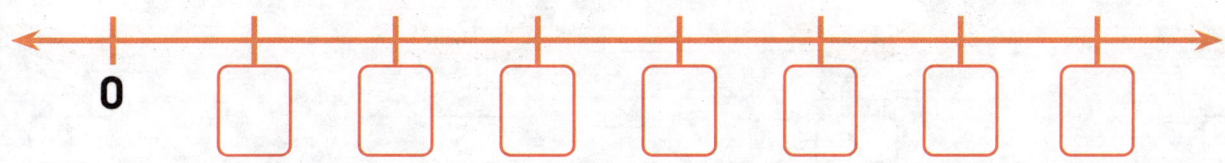

0

d. $\dfrac{6}{7}$, $\dfrac{4}{7}$, $\dfrac{3}{7}$, $\dfrac{8}{7}$, $\dfrac{1}{7}$, $\dfrac{5}{7}$, $\dfrac{7}{7}$, $\dfrac{2}{7}$

0

Count and Color

Count the colored seeds and write the fraction.

a.

b.

Write the fractions of the colored part.

a.

b.

c.

d.

e.

f.

g.

h.

Color the circle as per the given fraction.

a.  $\dfrac{1}{4}$

b.  $\dfrac{2}{3}$

c.  $\dfrac{5}{8}$

d.  $\dfrac{1}{2}$

e.  $\dfrac{7}{8}$

f.  $\dfrac{3}{8}$

g.  $\dfrac{1}{3}$

h.  $\dfrac{3}{4}$

Identify the Fraction

Match the figures with their fractions.

$$\frac{3}{8}$$

$$\frac{1}{8}$$

$$\frac{1}{4}$$

$$\frac{4}{9}$$

$$\frac{2}{8}$$

$$\frac{3}{16}$$

$$\frac{2}{4}$$

$$\frac{2}{6}$$

Fruity Fun

Jane saw 5 starfish and brought 3 home with her. What fraction of the starfish did she bring?

_____

Out of 10 tomatoes, Mike ate 6 tomatoes. What is the fraction of tomatoes that Mike ate?

_____

Color the grid according to the given fractions.

a.  $\frac{5}{10}$

b. $\frac{4}{10}$

c. $\frac{6}{10}$

d. $\frac{1}{10}$

e. $\frac{3}{10}$

f. $\frac{8}{10}$

g. $\frac{7}{10}$

h. $\frac{2}{10}$

Fruity Fractions

Color the fruits according to the given fractions.

a. $\dfrac{5}{7}$

b. $\dfrac{2}{5}$

c. $\dfrac{4}{6}$

d. $\dfrac{1}{5}$

e. $\dfrac{3}{7}$

Write the fraction according to the colored part of the fruit.

a.

b.

c.

d.

Color is the Key

Which is the bigger fraction in each pair?

a.
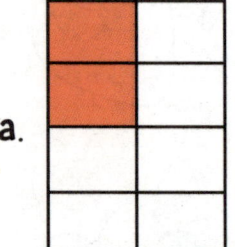 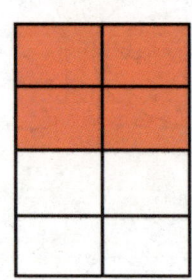

$$\frac{2}{8}$$ ☐ $$\frac{4}{8}$$

b.
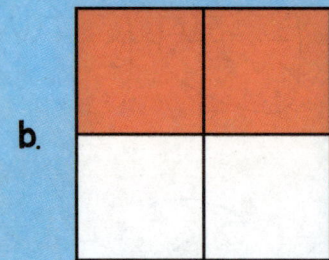 

$$\frac{2}{4}$$ ☐ $$\frac{3}{4}$$

c.
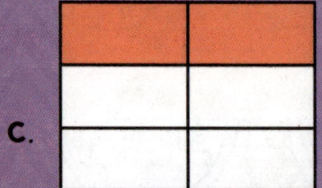 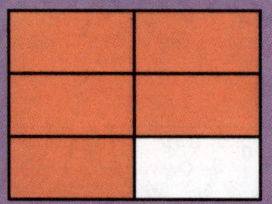

$$\frac{2}{6}$$ ☐ $$\frac{5}{6}$$

d.
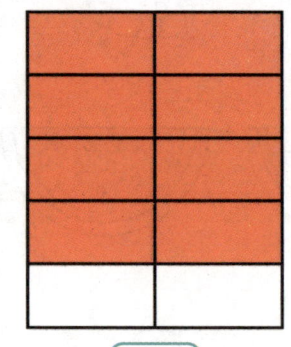

$$\frac{8}{10}$$ ☐ $$\frac{4}{10}$$

Count the colored part and write the fractions.

a.

$$\frac{}{8}$$

b.

$$\frac{}{8}$$

c.

$$\frac{}{8}$$

d.
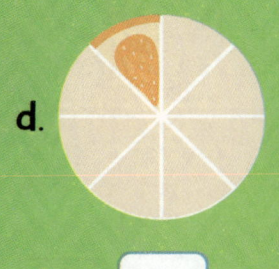

$$\frac{}{8}$$

e.

$$\frac{}{8}$$

How many Pizza Slices?

Circle the fraction that resembles the eaten pizza slices.

a.  $\frac{2}{6}$ $\frac{1}{6}$ $\frac{5}{6}$ $\frac{3}{6}$

b.  $\frac{2}{6}$ $\frac{3}{6}$ $\frac{6}{6}$ $\frac{4}{6}$

c.  $\frac{3}{6}$ $\frac{1}{6}$ $\frac{5}{6}$ $\frac{4}{6}$

d.  $\frac{3}{6}$ $\frac{2}{6}$ $\frac{1}{6}$ $\frac{5}{6}$

Tasty Watermelons

Match the watermelons with their fraction. One has been done for you.

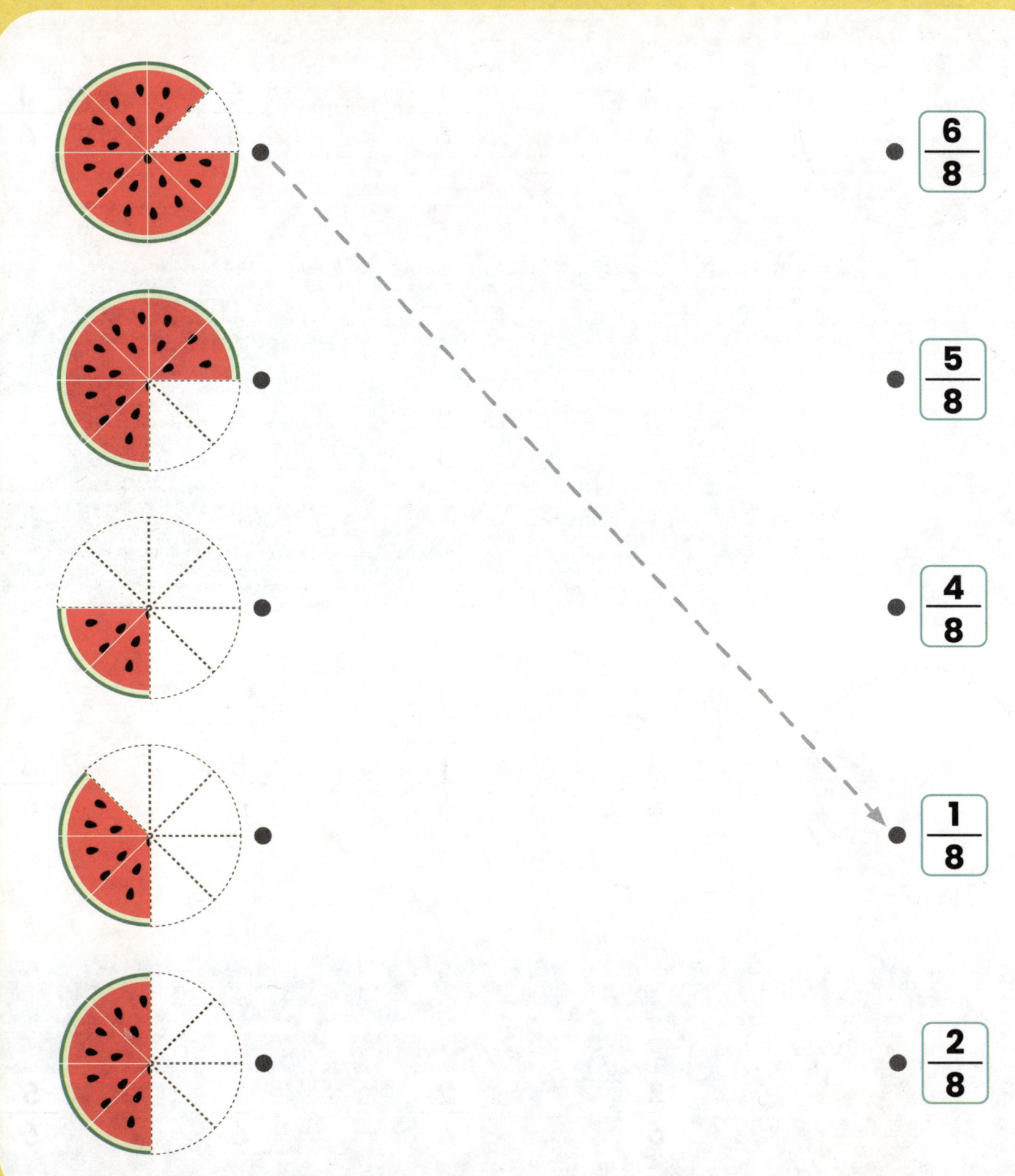

Let's Party

Count the stripes on the straw that are in the liquid and complete the fraction.

a.

$$\frac{}{16}$$

b.

$$\frac{}{16}$$

c.

$$\frac{}{16}$$

d.

$$\frac{}{16}$$

Color the gift boxes according to the given fractions.

a.

$$\frac{3}{4}$$

b.

$$\frac{1}{2}$$

c.

$$\frac{5}{8}$$

d.

$$\frac{2}{4}$$

e.

$$\frac{1}{2}$$

f.

$$\frac{2}{3}$$

Greater Fraction

Observe the stars, write the fraction of the colored part of the star and choose which fraction is bigger.

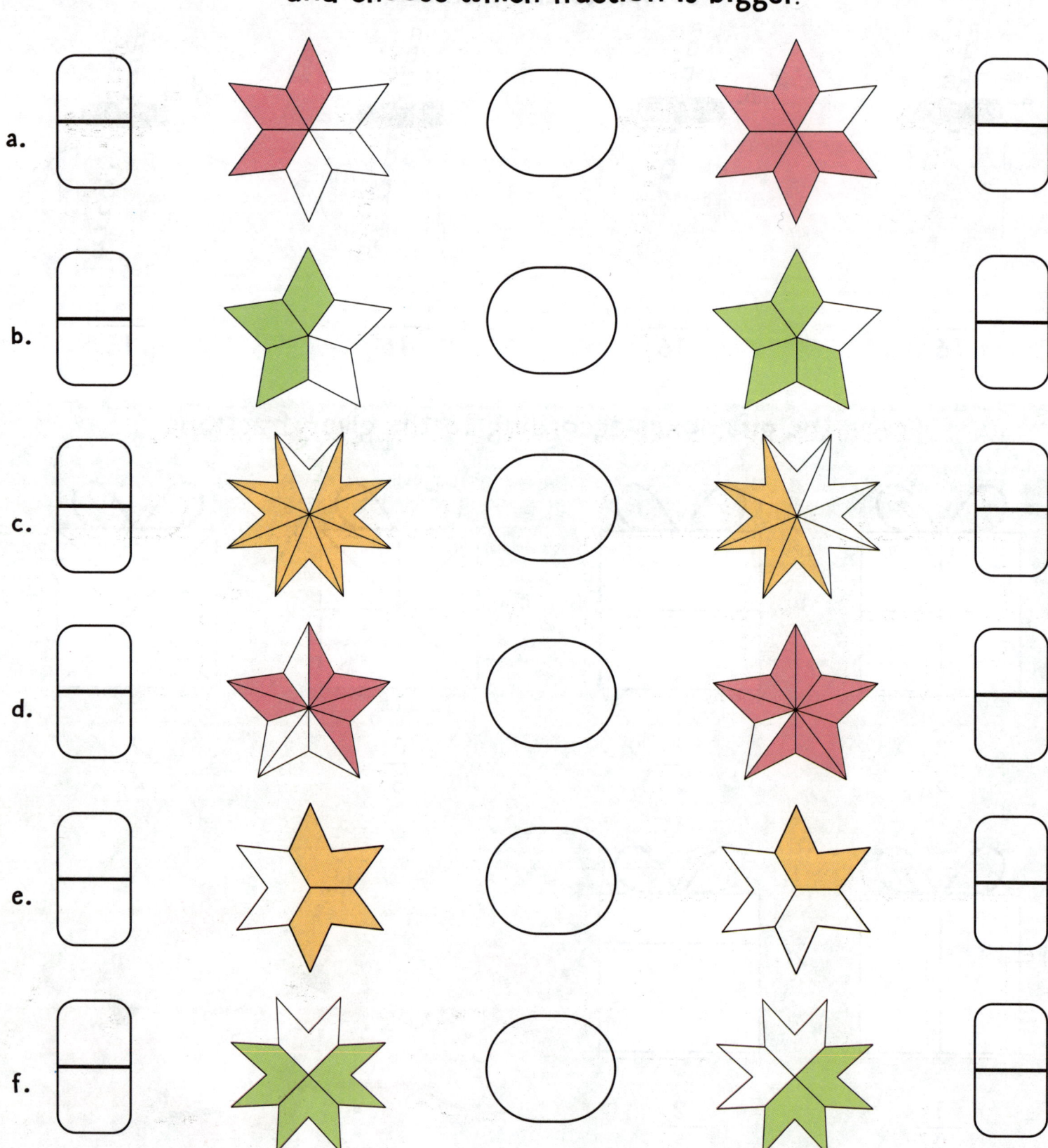

a.

b.

c.

d.

e.

f.

Fraction Fun

Color the sections of circle according to the colored part of the bar and write the fraction.

a.

b.

c.

d.

Write the fraction according to the colored part of the boards.

a.

b.

c.

d.

e.

f.

Compare the fractions.

a. $\dfrac{1}{13}$ ☐ $\dfrac{7}{13}$

b. $\dfrac{4}{12}$ ☐ $\dfrac{2}{12}$

c. $\dfrac{3}{14}$ ☐ $\dfrac{2}{14}$

d. $\dfrac{6}{10}$ ☐ $\dfrac{3}{10}$

e. $\dfrac{1}{15}$ ☐ $\dfrac{3}{15}$

23

Color Fraction

Observe the figures and write the fractions of the colors in each figure.

a. $\dfrac{2}{7}$

b.

c.

d. $\dfrac{3}{13}$

Simplifying Fractions

What is Simplifying Fractions?
It means to write the lowest possible numerator and denominator of a fraction. This new fraction cannot be divided any more.

Count the colored part and write the fraction. Then, simplify it. One has been done for you.

a. $\dfrac{4}{8} = \dfrac{1}{2}$

b. $\dfrac{}{} = \dfrac{}{}$

c. $\dfrac{}{} = \dfrac{}{}$

Blooming Fractions

Simplify the given fractions. Match your answers with the fractions on the flowers. One has been done for you.

Matching Fractions

Look at the figures carefully and choose the correct fraction.

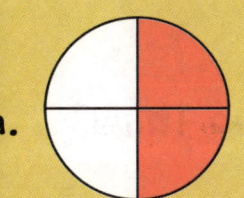 a.

$\dfrac{2}{4}$ 1.　$\dfrac{1}{2}$ 2.　$\dfrac{8}{4}$ 3.

d.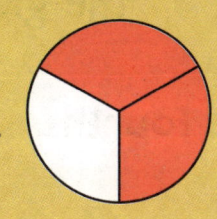

$\dfrac{4}{2}$ 1.　$\dfrac{1}{1}$ 2.　$\dfrac{2}{3}$ 3.

b.

$\dfrac{3}{6}$ 1.　$\dfrac{2}{3}$ 2.　$\dfrac{4}{2}$ 3.

e.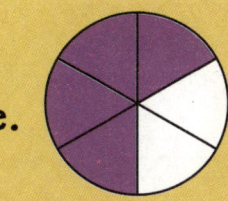

$\dfrac{4}{6}$ 1.　$\dfrac{5}{6}$ 2.　$\dfrac{2}{3}$ 3.

c.

$\dfrac{6}{8}$ 1.　$\dfrac{1}{3}$ 2.　$\dfrac{3}{4}$ 3.

f.

$\dfrac{2}{7}$ 1.　$\dfrac{5}{6}$ 2.　$\dfrac{4}{7}$ 3.

Match the fractions on the tree with their simplified forms on the ornaments.

27

Understanding Fractions

Observe the colored part and tick (✓) the correct option for the given shapes.

a. 
- ○ Three Fourth
- ○ Two Fourth

b. 
- ○ Two Third
- ○ One Third

c. 
- ○ One Fifth
- ○ Four Fifth

d. 
- ○ Two Fifth
- ○ Three Fifth

e. 
- ○ One Fifth
- ○ Two Fifth

f. 
- ○ One Third
- ○ Two Third

There are 20 books and 5 children who want to read them. What fraction of books should each of them get?

___

21 people want to buy muffins at a bakery but there are only 7 muffins left. What fraction of muffins would each of them get?

___

Increasing Order

Put these in order from smallest to the largest.

a. $\dfrac{1}{5}$ $\dfrac{2}{5}$ $\dfrac{4}{5}$ $\dfrac{6}{5}$ $\dfrac{3}{5}$ $\dfrac{5}{5}$ _____

b. $\dfrac{6}{6}$ $\dfrac{1}{6}$ $\dfrac{3}{6}$ $\dfrac{5}{6}$ $\dfrac{4}{6}$ $\dfrac{2}{6}$ _____

c. $\dfrac{3}{8}$ $\dfrac{2}{8}$ $\dfrac{7}{8}$ $\dfrac{4}{8}$ $\dfrac{1}{8}$ $\dfrac{5}{8}$ _____

d. $\dfrac{2}{7}$ $\dfrac{4}{7}$ $\dfrac{6}{7}$ $\dfrac{7}{7}$ $\dfrac{5}{7}$ $\dfrac{3}{7}$ _____

What is the fraction of the fruits and vegetables in each group?

1.

a. Apple $\dfrac{2}{7}$ b. Mango  c. Orange

2.

a. Tomato  b. Corn  c. Pumpkin

Matching Fun

Match the fractions and the figures by following the correct pattern.

$$\dfrac{18}{6} \qquad \dfrac{20}{4} \qquad \dfrac{18}{3} \qquad \dfrac{12}{3} \qquad \dfrac{8}{1} \qquad \dfrac{10}{5}$$

a.

b.

c.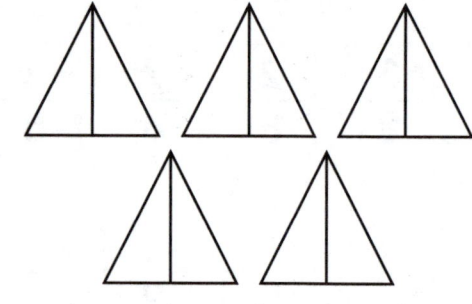

d.

e.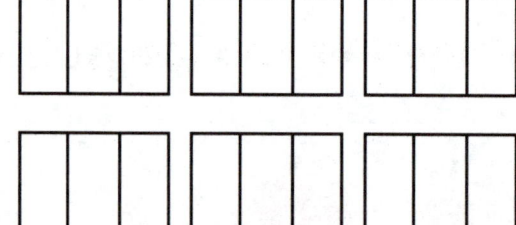

f.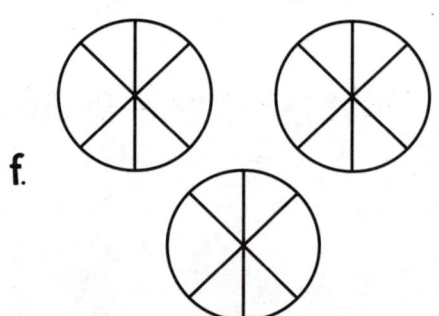

Write the fractions according to the fruits in each section of the cake.

a.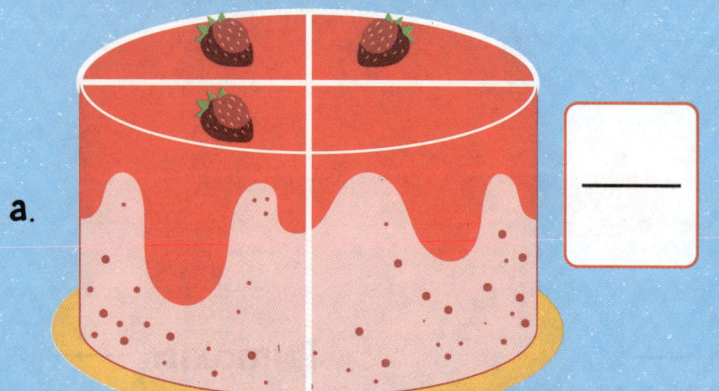

b.

Gift Bag

There are 6 gift bags. Read carefully and write the fractions.

a.

1. How many lollipops are there?_____

2. How many go in each gift bag? _____

3. What fraction of lollipops go in each bag?

—

b.

1. How many squares of chocolate are there? _____

2. How much goes in each bag? _____ Pieces

3. What fraction of the bar go in each bag?

—

c.

1. How many caps are there? _____

2. How many go in each gift bag? _____

3. What fraction of the caps go in each bag?

—

Draw the contents of the gift bag.

Draw lines and divide this cake equally among 4 people.

Color Fractions

Look carefully at the figures given on the Left. Color the blank figure based on them.

a.  +  =

b. 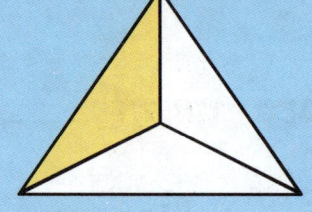 +  =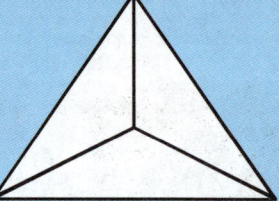

c.  +  =

d.  +  =

e.  +  =

Adding Fractions

Write the fractions of the colored part. Add them, write the new fraction and color the pumpkins accordingly.

a. 
$$\frac{}{5} \quad + \quad \frac{}{5} \quad = \quad \frac{}{5}$$

b. 
$$\frac{}{5} \quad + \quad \frac{}{5} \quad = \quad \frac{}{5}$$

Add the fractions and color the pyramid according to your answer.

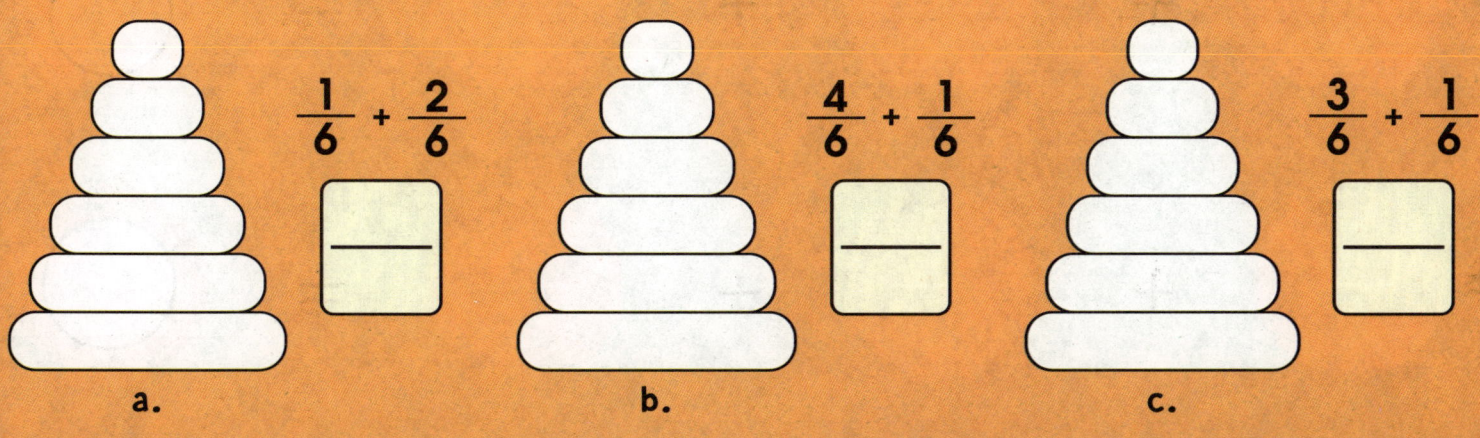

$$\frac{1}{6} + \frac{2}{6} \qquad \frac{4}{6} + \frac{1}{6} \qquad \frac{3}{6} + \frac{1}{6}$$

a.   b.   c.

33

Figures and Fractions

Solve the following sums.

a.  $\dfrac{1}{8}$ +  $\dfrac{6}{8}$ =  $\dfrac{7}{8}$

b.  $\dfrac{}{}$ +  $\dfrac{}{}$ =  $\dfrac{}{}$

c.  $\dfrac{}{}$ +  $\dfrac{}{}$ =  $\dfrac{}{}$

Add the fractions and write the answer.

a.  $\dfrac{3}{9}$ +  $\dfrac{4}{9}$ +  $\dfrac{1}{9}$ =

b.  $\dfrac{1}{5}$ +  $\dfrac{1}{5}$ +  $\dfrac{2}{5}$ =

Fruity Fractions

Add the fractions and color the fruits according to the answer.

a.

$$\frac{2}{8} + \frac{3}{8} = \underline{\quad}$$

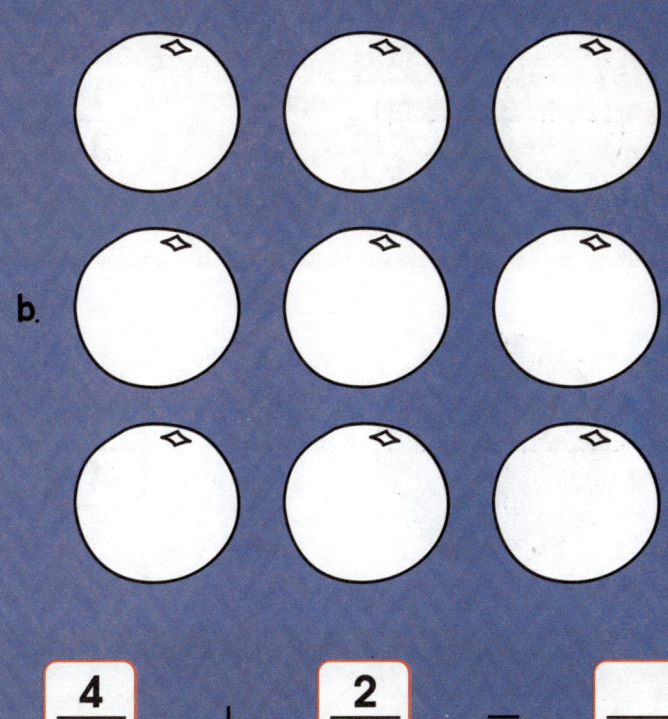

b.

$$\frac{4}{9} + \frac{2}{9} = \underline{\quad}$$

Split the given fractions into two. Color the fruits according to the given answer.

a.

$$\underline{\quad} + \underline{\quad} = \frac{3}{6}$$

b.

$$\underline{\quad} + \underline{\quad} = \frac{4}{7}$$

Subtracting Fractions

Subtract the fractions and write the answers.

a.  − $\dfrac{1}{3}$  = $\dfrac{2}{3}$

b. 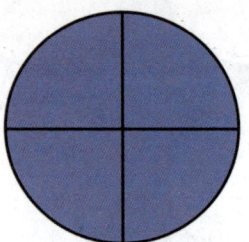 − $\dfrac{1}{4}$ 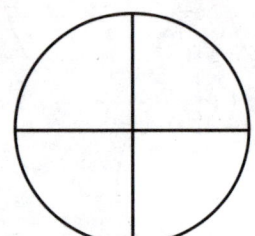 =

c.  − $\dfrac{5}{8}$ 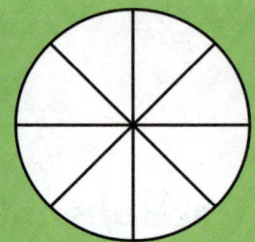 =

d. 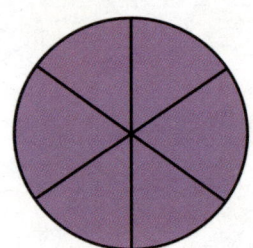 − $\dfrac{3}{6}$ 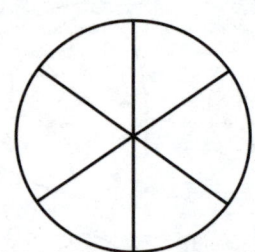 =

e. 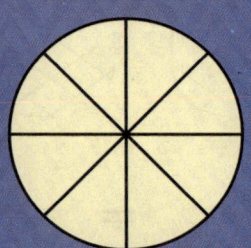 − $\dfrac{3}{8}$ 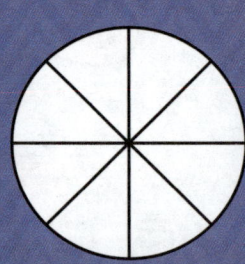 =

Bugs and Fraction

Subtract the fractions and color the insects accordingly.

a.

b.

$$\frac{9}{9} - \frac{4}{9} = \boxed{}$$

$$\frac{7}{8} - \frac{5}{8} = \boxed{}$$

c.

d.

$$\frac{5}{6} - \boxed{} = \frac{3}{6}$$

$$\frac{3}{7} - \boxed{} = \frac{1}{7}$$

Fraction Fun

Add the fractions.

a. $\frac{3}{4}$ + $\frac{2}{4}$ = $\frac{5}{4}$

b. $\frac{2}{6}$ + $\frac{2}{6}$ = ◯

c. $\frac{4}{8}$ + $\frac{5}{8}$ = ◯

Subtract the fractions.

a. $\frac{3}{6}$ - $\frac{2}{6}$ =

b. $\frac{6}{9}$ - $\frac{4}{9}$ =

c. $\frac{5}{8}$ - $\frac{3}{8}$ =

Find the missing fraction.

a. $\frac{5}{10}$ + ◯ = $\frac{7}{10}$

b. ◯ + $\frac{2}{8}$ = $\frac{6}{8}$

c. $\frac{3}{8}$ + $\frac{4}{8}$ = ◯

d. ◯ + $\frac{8}{12}$ = $\frac{10}{12}$

Solve the fraction sums.

a. $\frac{3}{5}$ - $\frac{2}{5}$ = ◯

b. $\frac{10}{15}$ + $\frac{3}{15}$ = ◯

c. $\frac{10}{9}$ - $\frac{4}{9}$ = ◯

d. $\frac{6}{8}$ + $\frac{2}{8}$ = ◯

38

Simple Fractions

Solve the fraction sum and write the answer.

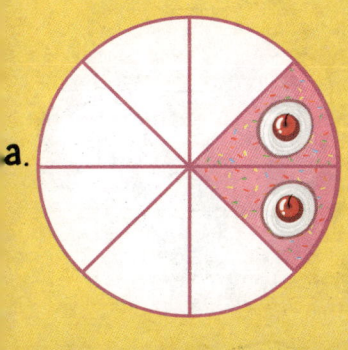

a. □/□ + □/□

= □/□

b. 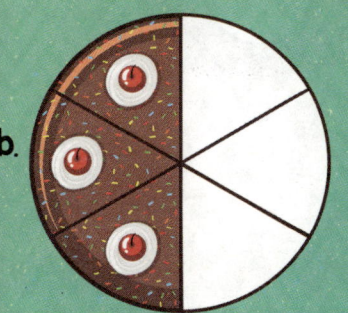 +

□/□ + □/□

= □/□

Solve the fractions and color the fruits according to the answer.

a. $\dfrac{7}{8}$ - $\dfrac{3}{8}$ = □/□

b. $\dfrac{5}{6}$ - $\dfrac{3}{6}$ = □/□

c. $\dfrac{6}{7}$ - $\dfrac{4}{7}$ = □/□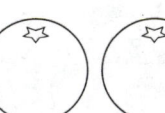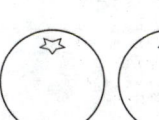

c. $\dfrac{7}{8}$ - $\dfrac{5}{8}$ = □/□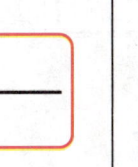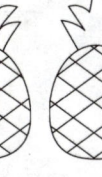

39

Simplifying Fractions

Simplify the answers of each fraction sum.

$\frac{2}{8}$ + $\frac{2}{8}$ = $\frac{4}{8}$

a.

$\frac{10}{9}$ + $\frac{2}{9}$ = $\frac{12}{9}$

b.

$\frac{6}{12}$ + $\frac{4}{12}$ = $\frac{10}{12}$

c.

Write the given fractions in the simplest manner.

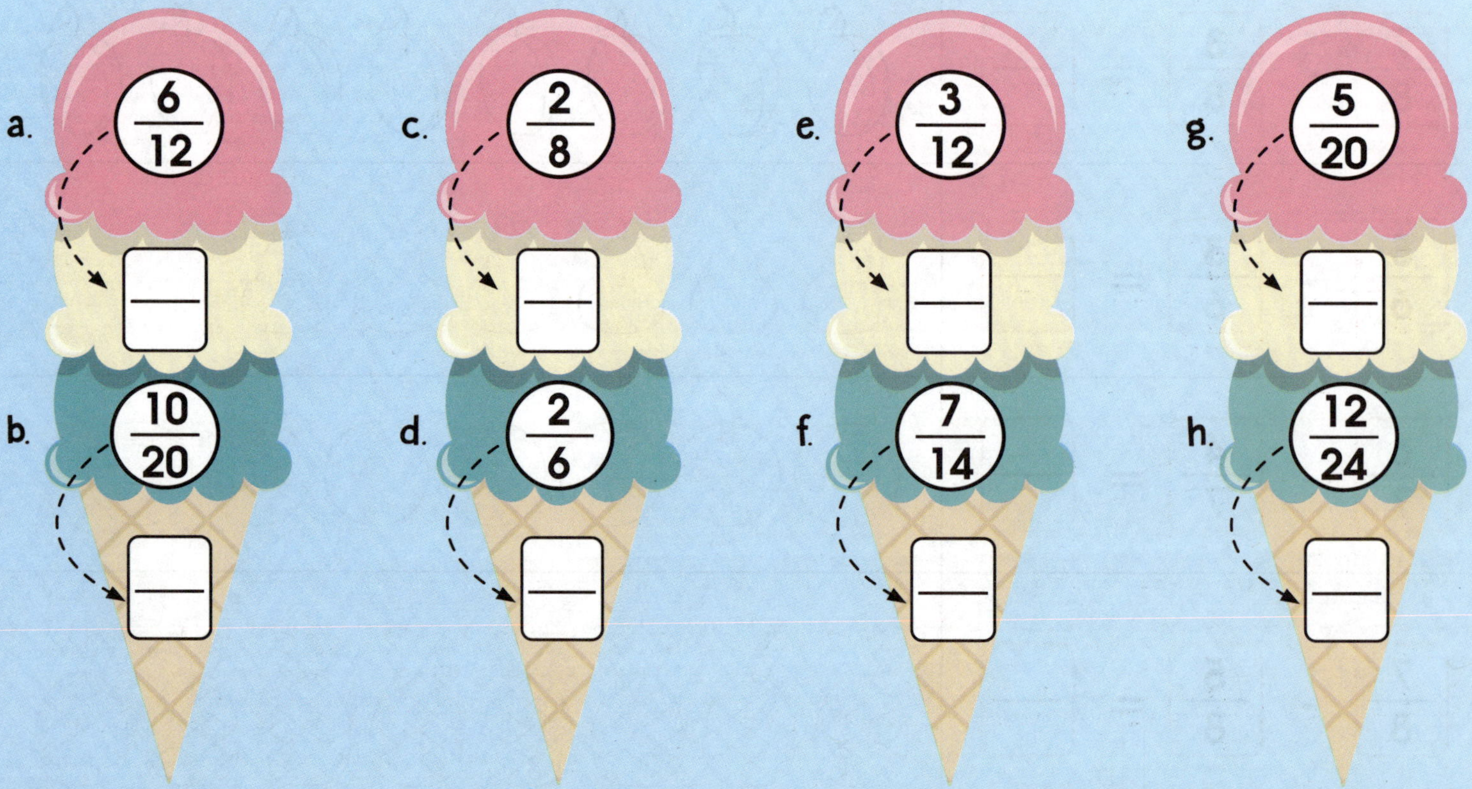

a. $\frac{6}{12}$

b. $\frac{10}{20}$

c. $\frac{2}{8}$

d. $\frac{2}{6}$

e. $\frac{3}{12}$

f. $\frac{7}{14}$

g. $\frac{5}{20}$

h. $\frac{12}{24}$

Color Addition

Color the missing fractions. First one is done for you.

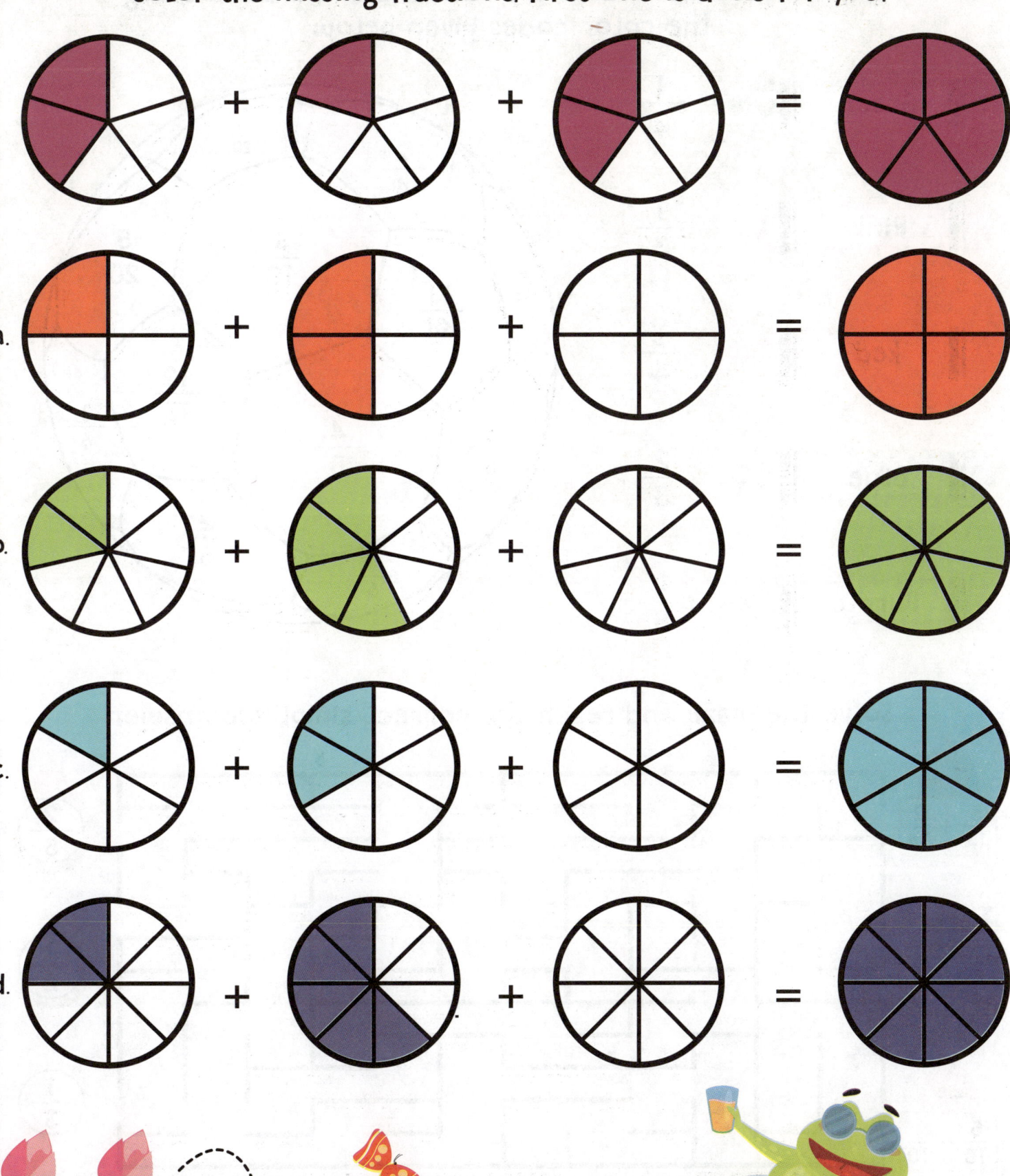

Simplify and Color

Simplify the fractions in the ball and color them using the color codes given below.

a.  Green $\dfrac{1}{2}$

b. Pink $\dfrac{1}{3}$

c.  Red $\dfrac{1}{4}$

d. Blue $\dfrac{2}{3}$

e. Purple $\dfrac{2}{5}$

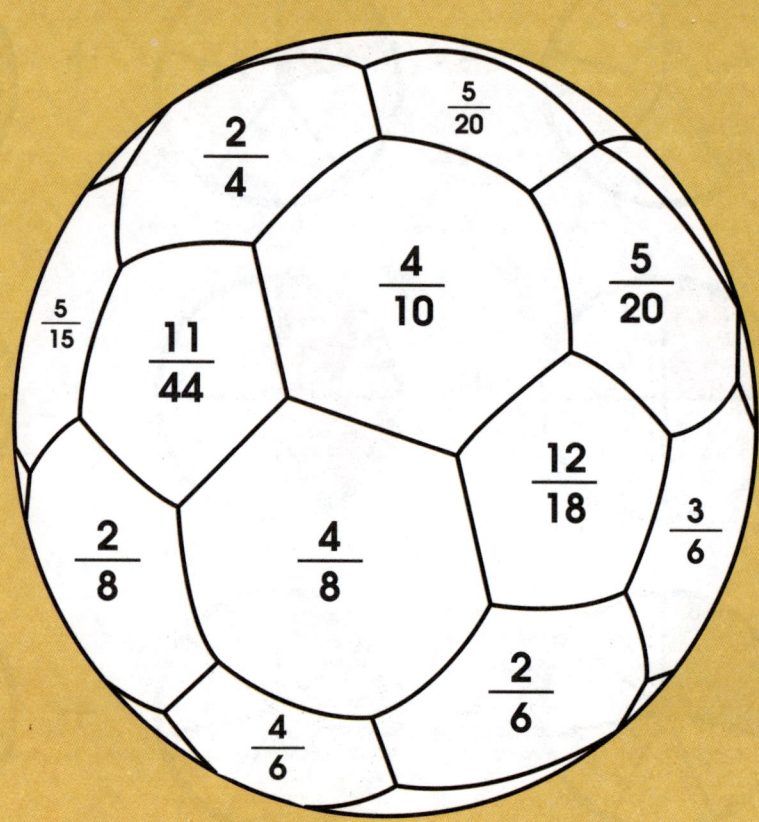

Solve the maze and reach the correct simplified answer.

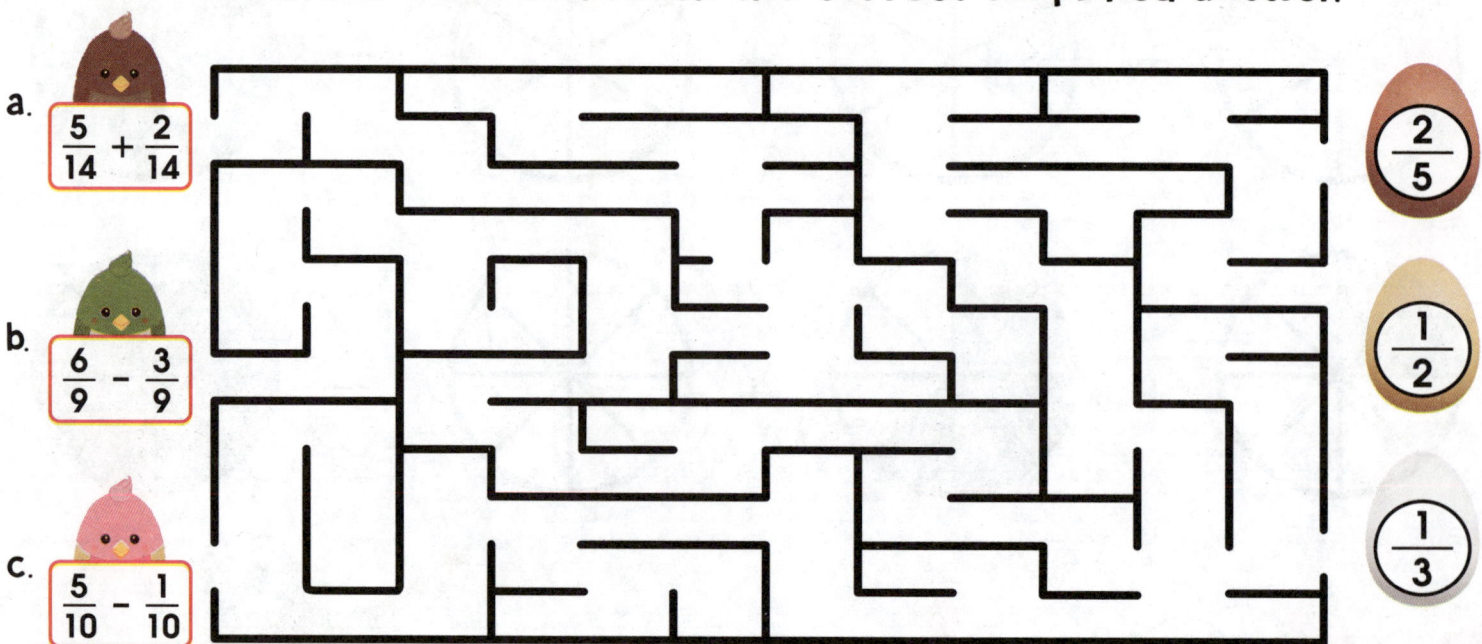

a. $\dfrac{5}{14} + \dfrac{2}{14}$

b. $\dfrac{6}{9} - \dfrac{3}{9}$

c. $\dfrac{5}{10} - \dfrac{1}{10}$

$\dfrac{2}{5}$

$\dfrac{1}{2}$

$\dfrac{1}{3}$

Practicing Fractions

Solve the given fractions.

a. $\dfrac{3}{12} + \dfrac{4}{12} = \overline{}$

b. $\dfrac{6}{10} - \boxed{} = \dfrac{1}{10}$

c. $\dfrac{4}{11} + \boxed{} = \dfrac{5}{11}$

d. $\boxed{} - \dfrac{6}{10} = \dfrac{9}{10}$

e. $\dfrac{14}{12} + \dfrac{2}{12} = \overline{}$

f. $\dfrac{5}{8} + \dfrac{2}{8} = \overline{}$

g. $\boxed{} - \dfrac{4}{13} = \dfrac{3}{13}$

h. $\dfrac{2}{5} - \dfrac{1}{5} = \overline{}$

i. $\dfrac{1}{13} + \dfrac{5}{13} = \overline{}$

j. $\overline{} + \dfrac{5}{22} = \dfrac{17}{22}$

Simplify the Word Problems

Austin had 12 Skittles. 6 were yellow. 3 were orange, and 3 were red. What fraction of his Skittles were yellow?

Mr. Martin bought a medium pizza which was cut into 10 slices. If his son Ryan ate four slices, what fraction of the pizza was left?

In a hotel there are 20 rooms. Out of them 13 rooms were occupied. Write the fraction of rooms that are unoccupied.

Anne has a box of 9 chocolates. She took 5 of them. She gave the rest to her brother. What fraction of the chocolates were eaten by her brother?

Grace has 10 pairs of socks. Half of them are torn. What fraction of socks are good to use?

A basket contains 15 balls. 10 of them were yellow and the rest were blue. What is the fraction of blue balls in the basket?

A rose plant has 15 roses on it. 6 of them have fully bloomed and the rest of them are buds. What fraction of roses are buds?

A pumpkin pie was cut into 6 pieces. Out of that 5 pieces were eaten. What fraction of the pie was left behind?

Who Comes First?

Red or Blue, which car will be able to reach the center? Be mindful, to avoid the red circles. Solve the sum written on the car that reaches the green zone in the space given below.

$$\frac{10}{20} + \frac{5}{20}$$

$$\frac{5}{15} - \frac{2}{15}$$

Practice Fractions

Practice fractions of addition and subtraction.

a. $\dfrac{4}{15} + \dfrac{3}{15} = \dfrac{}{}$

b. $\dfrac{3}{20} + \dfrac{2}{20} = \dfrac{}{}$

c. $\dfrac{2}{14} - \dfrac{1}{14} = \dfrac{}{}$

d. $\dfrac{7}{18} + \dfrac{2}{18} = \dfrac{}{}$

e. $\dfrac{11}{17} - \dfrac{2}{17} = \dfrac{}{}$

f. $\dfrac{4}{9} - \dfrac{2}{9} = \dfrac{}{}$

g. $\dfrac{7}{19} - \dfrac{5}{19} = \dfrac{}{}$

h. $\dfrac{5}{14} - \dfrac{3}{14} = \dfrac{}{}$

i. $\dfrac{3}{12} + \dfrac{11}{12} = \dfrac{}{}$

j. $\dfrac{2}{9} + \dfrac{5}{9} = \dfrac{}{}$

k. $\dfrac{4}{13} + \dfrac{10}{13} = \dfrac{}{}$

L. $\dfrac{10}{15} + \dfrac{2}{15} = \dfrac{}{}$

Answers

Page 2

a) 3/5,
b) 5/8,
c) 6/10,
d) 7/9

Page 3

a) denominator,
b) numerator,
c) denominator,
d) denominator,
e) numerator

Page 5

b) 1/5,
c) 3/5,
d) 4/6,
e) 2/6

Page 8

a) 5/8, b) 2/8,
c) 3/8, d) 6/8;

a) 2/8<3/8,
b) 1/9<7/9

Page 10

a) 4/8, b) 8/8,
c) 6/8, d) 3/8,
e) 8/8, f) 8/8;

a) 6/ 7, b) 9/12,
c) 6/6, d) 3/3

Page 11

a) 4/5,
b) 4/6,
c) 7/7,
d) 5/8

Page 12

a) 4/6,
b) 3/5,
c) 2/5,
d) 3/4,
e) 1/4,
f) 2/4

Page 14

a) 4/9, b) 12/22;

a) 1/4, b) 3/4,
c) 6/7, d) 3/7,
e) 2/4, f) 1/4,
g) 5/7, h) 2/7

Page 16

3/5;
6/10

Page 17

a) 6/8,
b) 2/8,
c) 4/8,
d) 3/8

Page 18

a) 4/8, b) 3/4,
c) 5/6, d) 8/10;

a) 2/8, b) 3/8,
c) 6/8, d) 1/8,
e) 7/8

Page 19

b) 2/6,
c) 4/6,
d) 3/6

Page 21

a) 6/16, b) 4/16,
c) 2/16, d) 7/16

Page 22

a) 3/6<5/6,
b) 3/5<4/5,
c) 7/8>4/8,
d) 6/10<9/10,
e) 2/3>1/3,
f) 3/4>2/4

Page 23

a) 3/4, b) 5/8,
c) 2/3, d) 1/3;

a) 3/6, b) 5/8,
c) 2/6, d) 2/4,
e) 1/2, f) 2/3

Page 24

a) 1/7, 2/7, 2/7,
b) 3/14, 5/14, 2/14,
4/14,
c) 3/7, 2/7, 1/7, 1/7,
d) 4/13, 3/13, 3/13

Page 25

b) 1/4,
c) 2/5

Page 26

6/18=1/3, 3/6=1/2,
5/10=1/2, 5/15=1/3,
7/14=1/2, 4/8=1/2,
4/16=1/4, 4/12=1/3,
3/9=1/3, 3/12=1/4,
2/8=1/4, 2/6=1/3,
5/20=1/4, 7/21=1/3

Page 27

a) 1, b) 1,
c) 1, d) 3,
e) 1, f) 3;

a) 16/10=8/5,
b) 9/6=3/2,
c) 4/6=2/3,

Page 27

d) 2/6=1/3,
e) 8/14=4/7,
f) 20/12=5/3,
g) 5/10 =1/2,
h) 14/35=2/5,
i) 10/2=5,
j) 5/5=1

Page 28

a) three fourth,
b) one third,
c) four fifth,
d) two fifth,
e) one fifth,
f) two third;

20/5; 7/21

Page 29

b) 3/7, c) 2/7;

a) 3/7, b) 1/7,
c) 3/7

Page 30

b) 12/3, c) 10/5,
d) 20/4, e) 18/6,
f) 18/3;

a) 3/4, b) 6/8

Page 31

a) 6, 1, 1/6,
b) 12, 2, 2/12
c) 12, 2, 2/12

Page 33

a) 1/5+2/5=3/5
b) 3/5+1/5=4/5;

a) 3/6
b) 5/6
c) 4/6

Page 34

b) 3/8+4/ 8=7/8
c) 4/8+2/8=6/8;

a) 8/9, b) 4/5

Page 35

a) 5/8, b) 6/9;

a) 2/6+1/6,
b) 2/7+2/7

Page 36

b) 3/4,
c) 3/8,
d) 3/6,
e) 5/8

Page 37

a) 5/9,
b) 2/8,
c) 2/6,
d) 2/7

Page 38

b) 4/6, c) 9/8;

a) 1/6, b) 2/9, c) 2/8;

a) 2/10, b) 4/8,
c)7/8, d) 2/12;

Page 38

a) 1/5, b) 13/15,
c) 6/9, d) 8/8

Page 39

a) 2/8+2/8=4/8,
b) 3/6+2/6=5/6;

a) 4/8, b) 2/6,
c) 2/7, d) 2/8

Page 40

a) 1/2, b) 4/3, c) 5/6;

a) 1/2, b) 1/2,
c) 1/4, d) 1/3,
e) 1/4, f) 1/2,
g) 1/4, h) 1/2

Page 43

a) 7/12, b) 5/10,
c) 1/11, d) 15/10,
e) 16/12, f) 7/8,
g) 7/13, h) 1/5,
i) 6/13, j) 12/22

Page 44

1/2; 7/20; 1/2; 3/5;
3/5; 4/9; 1/3; 1/6

Page 46

a) 7/15, b) 5/20,
c) 1/14, d) 9/18,
e) 9/17, f) 2/9,
g) 2/19, h) 2/14,
i) 14/12, j) 7/9,
k) 14/13, l) 12/15